Have A Good Bundt
on Me

25 Amazing Bundt Cake Recipes You Can
Enjoy Any Time

BY

MOLLY MILLS

Copyright © 2019 by Molly Mills

License Notes

An Amazing Offer for Buying My Book!

Thank you very much for purchasing my books! As a token of my appreciation, I would like to extend an amazing offer to you! When you have subscribed with your e-mail address, you will have the opportunity to get free and discounted e-books that will show up in your inbox daily. You will also receive reminders before an offer expires so you never miss out. With just little effort on your part, you will have access to the newest and most informative books at your fingertips. This is all part of the VIP treatment when you subscribe below.

SIGN ME UP: *https://molly.gr8.com*

Table of Contents

Delicious Bundt Cake

Recipes

AAAAAAAAAAAAAAAAAAAAAAAAAAAAAAAAAAAAAAAAAAAAAAAAAAAA

Recipe 1: Lemon Bundt Cake

This is a delicious and refreshing Bundt cake that you can make during the summer holiday season. One bite and you will want to make it as often as possible.

Yield: 10 Servings

Cooking Time: 1 Hour and 5 Minutes

Ingredients for the cake:

- 1, 16 -ounce box of lemon cake mix
- 1, 3.4 -ounce box of vanilla pudding, instant
- ½ cup of sour cream
- ¾ cup of vegetable oil
- ¾ cup of warm water
- ½ cup of sugar, granulated
- 4 eggs, large
- 1 tablespoon of lemon zest, fresh
- 3 tablespoons of lemon juice, fresh

Ingredients for the frosting:

- 8 -ounces of cream cheese, soft
- 2 cups of sugar, powdered
- 1 tablespoon of lemon zest, fresh
- 1 teaspoon of lemon juice, fresh

AAAAAAAAAAAAAAAAAAAAAAAAAAAAAAAAAAAAAAAAAAAAAAAAAAA

Instructions:

1. Heat up the oven to 350 degrees.

2. While the oven is heating up use a large bowl and add in all the ingredients for the cake. Stir well to mix.

3. Pour the batter into a large Bundt pan.

4. Place into the oven to bake for 50 minutes or until completely baked through. Remove and allow to sit in the pan to cool for 5 minutes before inverting onto a wire rack to cool completely.

5. Meanwhile prepare the frosting. To do this use a medium bowl and add in the cream cheese, powdered sugar, fresh lemon zest and fresh lemon juice. Beat with an electric mixer on the highest setting until creamy in consistency.

6. Pour the frosting over the top of the cake, making sure to spread it evenly on the surface.

7. Garnish with the fresh lemon zest and serve.

Recipe 2: Buttermilk Breakfast Bundt Cake

Just as the name implies, this is the perfect Bundt cake to prepare for an early morning breakfast treat. Best of all you can take a slice on the go with you.

Yield: 12 Servings

Cooking Time: 1 Hour and 40 Minutes

Ingredients for the cake:

- 1, 18 ½ -ounce pack of white cake mix
- 1 cup of buttermilk
- ½ cup of butter, melted
- 5 eggs, large
- 3 tablespoons of brown sugar, light and packed
- 2 teaspoons of cinnamon
- Shortening
- 1 tablespoon of sugar, granulated

Ingredients for the buttermilk and vanilla icing:

- 1 cup of sugar powdered
- 1 tablespoon of butter, melted
- 1 teaspoon of pure vanilla
- 1 to 2 tablespoons of buttermilk

AAAAAAAAAAAAAAAAAAAAAAAAAAAAAAAAAAAAAAAAAAAAAAAAAAA

Instructions:

1. First heat up the oven to 350 degrees.

2. While the oven is heating up add the white cake mix, buttermilk and melted butter to a large bowl. Beat with an electric mixer on the highest setting until blended. Add in the eggs and beat to incorporate.

3. Add the light brown sugar and cinnamon to a small bowl. Stir well until evenly mixed.

4. Grease a large Bundt cake pan with the shortening. Sprinkle the granulated sugar into the pan generously.

5. Pour 1/3 of the batter into the prepared Bundt pan. Sprinkle the brown sugar mixture over the batter. Top off with the remaining batter.

6. Place into the oven to bake for 45 minutes or until you see the cake is completely baked through (can be checked using a toothpick). Remove and allow to cool in the pan for 10 minutes. Remove from the pan and transfer to a wire rack to completely cool.

7. While the cake is cooling, make the icing. To do this add all the ingredients for the vanilla icing to a medium bowl. Whisk until smooth in consistency. Pour over the cooled cake and serve.

Recipe 3: Praline Bundt Cake

This delicious Bundt cake will get rave reviews within your home. It is a cake that is packed full of delicious flavor and is incredibly moist, making it a truly delicious Southern cake that you will love.

Yield: 12 Servings

Cooking Time: 2 Hours and 55 Minutes

Ingredients for the cake:

- 1 cup of pecans, chopped
- 1 cup of butter, soft
- 1, 8 -ounce pack of cream cheese, soft
- 1, 16 -ounce pack of dark sugar, light and packed
- 4 eggs, large
- 2 ½ cups all-purpose flour
- ½ teaspoons of baking soda
- ¼ teaspoons of salt
- 1 teaspoon of baking powder
- 1, 8 -ounce container of sour cream
- 2 teaspoons of pure vanilla

Ingredients for the praline icing:

- 1 cup of brown sugar, light and packed
- ½ cup of butter
- ¼ cup of milk, whole
- 1 cup of sugar, powdered
- 1 teaspoon of pure vanilla

Ingredients for the sugared pecans:

- 1 egg white, large
- 4 cups of pecans, cut into halves
- 1/3 cup of sugar, granulated
- 1/3 cup of brown sugar, light and packed

Instructions:

1. Place one cup of the chopped pecans onto a large baking sheet in a single layer. Place into the oven to bake at 350 degrees for 5 to 8 minutes or until lightly toasted. Remove and place onto a wire rack to cool completely.

2. Reduce the temperature of the oven to 325 degrees.

3. Add the butter and cream cheese to a medium bowl. Beat with an electric mixer on the highest setting until creamy in consistency. Add in the light brown sugar and eggs. Beat again to incorporate.

4. In a separate large bowl add in the all-purpose flour, a dash of salt and baking powder and soda. Stir well to mix. Add into the butter mixture along with the sour cream, lightly toasted pecans and pure vanilla. Beat on the lowest setting until evenly mixed.

5. Pour the batter into a large greased and floured Bundt pan.

6. Place into the oven to bake for 1 hour and 15 minutes or until the cake is fully baked through. Remove and set onto a wire rack to cool completely.

7. Meanwhile prepare the sugared pecans. To do this add the egg white to a small bowl. Beat with an electric mixer until foamy in consistency. Add in the pecans and fold gently to coat.

8. In a separate small bowl add in the granulated sugar and light brown sugar. Stir to mix and sprinkle over the pecans.

9. Spread the pecans over a large baking sheet. Place into the oven to bake for 20 minutes at 350 degrees or until lightly toasted. Remove and set aside to cool.

10. Then prepare the icing. To do this place a small saucepan over medium heat. Add in the whole milk, butter and light brown sugar. Whisk to mix and bring to a boil. Once boiling, allow to boil for 1 minute before removing from heat. Add in the powdered sugar and pure vanilla. Whisk until smooth in consistency. Set aside to thicken.

11. Pour the icing over the cooled cake. Sprinkle the sugared pecans over the top and serve.

Recipe 4: Strawberry Swirl Cream Cheese Bundt Cake

This is a cake that you can make for practically any occasion. Serve this with fresh strawberries for the tastiest results.

Yield: 12 Servings

Cooking Time: 2 Hours and 35 Minutes

List of Ingredients:

- 1 ½ cups of butter, soft
- 3 cups of sugar
- 1, 8 -ounce pack of cream cheese, soft
- 6 eggs, large
- 3 cups of all-purpose flour
- 1 teaspoon of almond extract
- ½ teaspoons of pure vanilla
- 2/3 cup of strawberry glaze
- 1 six-inch skewer, wooden

AAAAAAAAAAAAAAAAAAAAAAAAAAAAAAAAAAAAAAAAAAAAAAAAAA

Instructions:

1. Preheat the oven to 350 degrees.

2. While the oven is heating up add the butter to a large bowl. Beat with an electric mixer until creamy in consistency. Add in the sugar and continue to beat until fluffy in consistency.

3. Add in the cream cheese and eggs. Beat until thoroughly incorporated.

4. Add in the all-purpose flour and beat on the lowest setting until mixed. Add in the almond extract and pure vanilla. Beat again until combined.

5. Pour 1/3 of the batter into a large greased and floured Bundt pan. Add 8 teaspoons of the strawberry glaze over the batter. Swirl it around using a butter knife. Pour the remaining batter over the top.

6. Place into the oven to bake for 1 hour and 10 minutes or until completely baked through. Remove and allow to cool for about 10 minutes and then remove from the pan and transferring to a wire rack to cool completely.

Recipe 5: Hummingbird Bundt Cake

This hummingbird Bundt cake is packed with plenty of pineapple and cream cheese, making this a sweet and savory Bundt cake that will become popular in your household.

Yield: 10 to 12 Servings

Cooking Time: 3 Hours and 45 Minutes

Ingredients for the cake batter:

- 1 ½ cups of pecans, chopped
- 3 cups of flour, all-purpose
- 2 cups of sugar, granulated
- 1 teaspoon of baker's style baking soda
- 1 teaspoon of cinnamon, ground
- ½ teaspoons of salt
- 3 eggs, large and beaten lightly
- 1 ¾ cups of ripe bananas, mashed
- 1, 8 -ounce can of pineapple, crushed
- ¾ cup of canola oil
- 1 ½ teaspoons of pure vanilla

Ingredients for the glaze:

- 4 -ounces of cream cheese, soft
- 2 cups of sugar, powdered
- 1 teaspoon of pure vanilla
- 1 to 2 tablespoons of milk, whole

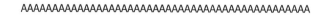

AAAAAAAAAAAAAAAAAAAAAAAAAAAAAAAAAAAAAAAAAAAAAAAAAAAAAA

Instructions:

1. The first thing that you will want to do is prepare the cake batter. To do this first preheat the oven to 350 degrees.

2. While the oven is heating up place the chopped pecans in a baking pan in a single layer. Place into the oven to roast for 8 to 10 minutes or until toasted. Remove and set aside.

3. Use a large bowl and add in the all-purpose flour, sugar, baking soda and cinnamon. Stir well to combine.

4. Add in the large eggs, mashed bananas, the can of crushed pineapple, oil and pure vanilla. Stir well until just moistened.

5. Sprinkle the toasted pecans into a large greased Bundt pan. Pour the batter over the pecans.

6. Place into the oven to bake for 1 hour to 1 hour and 10 minutes or until the cake is completely baked through. Remove and transfer to a wire rack to cool completely.

7. During this time make the glaze. To do this use a food processor and add in all of the ingredients for the glaze. Blend on the highest setting until smooth in consistency.

8. Pour the glaze immediately over the cooled Bundt pan. Sprinkle the remaining ½ cup of pecans over the top. Serve.

Recipe 6: Cheesecake Stuffed Chocolate Bundt Cake

If you wish to make a cake recipe that will impress your friends and family then this is the perfect cake dish for you. It is packed with a generous amount of chocolate and a cheesecake layer that I know you won't be able to resist.

Yield: 10 to 12 Servings

Cooking Time: 1 Hour and 20 Minutes

Ingredients for the filling:

- 8 -ounces of cream cheese
- ½ cup of sugar
- 1 egg, large
- 1 teaspoon of pure vanilla
- 2 teaspoons of flour, all-purpose
- Miniature chocolate chips, for garnish and optional

Ingredients for the cake:

- ¾ cup of cocoa, powdered and unsweetened
- 6 -ounces of chocolate, semisweet and chopped
- ¾ cup of water, boiling
- 1 ¾ cups of all-purpose flour
- 1 teaspoon of salt
- 1 teaspoon of baking soda
- 1 cup of sour cream
- 12 tablespoons of butter
- 2 cups of brown sugar, light and packed
- 1 tablespoon of pure vanilla
- 5 eggs, large

Ingredients for the glaze:

- ½ cup of heavy cream
- 2 teaspoons of corn syrup, light
- 4 -ounces of chocolate, semisweet and chopped

AAAAAAAAAAAAAAAAAAAAAAAAAAAAAAAAAAAAAAAAAAAAAAAAAAA

Instructions:

1. First heat up the oven to 350 degrees. While the oven is heating up grease a large Bundt pan and dust with flour lightly.

2. Then prepare the filling. To do this add the cream cheese and sugar to a large bowl. Beat until fluffy in consistency. Add in the large egg, pure vanilla and all-purpose flour. Beat again to mix and set aside.

3. Add the cocoa and chocolate to a medium bowl. Pour the boiling water over the top and cover. Allow to sit for 5 minutes before whisking until smooth in consistency. Allow to cool completely before adding in the sour cream. Whisk to incorporate.

4. Then make the cake. To do this use a large bowl and add in the butter, granulated sugar and pure vanilla. Beat with an electric mixer until fluffy in consistency. Add in the large eggs and stir to incorporate.

5. In a separate large bowl add in the all-purpose flour, dash of salt and baking soda. Stir to mix and add this mixture to the butter mixture. Add in the chocolate mixture and beat until evenly mixed.

6. Pour half of the batter into the prepared Bundt pan. Pour the cream cheese filling over the batter. Pour the remaining cake batter over the top.

7. Place into the oven to bake for 50 minutes or until completely baked through. Remove and allow to cool in the pan for 10 minutes before inverting and allowing to cool completely.

8. While the cake is cooling, make the glaze. To do this add the cream and light corn syrup to a small bowl. Microwave until it begins to boil. Add in the chocolate and allow to rest for 5 to 10 minutes or until melted. Whisk until smooth in consistency. Allow to sit for another 5 minutes to thicken.

9. Drizzle the glaze over the top of the cake. Garnish with the chocolate chips and serve.

Recipe 7: Triple Chocolate

Buttermilk Bundt Cake

This is the ultimate Bundt cake for all of the chocoholics out there. Smothered in a mouthwatering glaze, I know you will want to make this for every special occasion.

Yield: 10 to 12 Servings

Cooking Time: 4 Hours and 25 Minutes

Ingredients for the cake:

- 2 cups of all-purpose flour
- ¾ cup of cocoa, unsweetened
- ½ teaspoons of baking powder
- 1 teaspoon of salt
- 1 ½ cups of butter, soft
- 3 cups of sugar, granulated
- 5 eggs, large
- 1 ¼ cups of buttermilk
- 2 teaspoons of espresso, instant
- 2 teaspoons of pure vanilla
- 1 cup of cacao, bittersweet
- Shortening, for greasing

Ingredients for the chocolate glaze:

- ¾ cup of chocolate morsels, semi-sweet
- 3 tablespoons of butter
- 1 tablespoon of corn syrup, light
- ½ teaspoons of pure vanilla

Ingredients for the buttermilk glaze:

- 1 cup of sugar, powdered
- 1 to 2 tablespoons of buttermilk
- ¼ teaspoons of pure vanilla

AAAAAAAAAAAAAAAAAAAAAAAAAAAAAAAAAAAAAAAAAAAAAAAAAA

Instructions:

1. First preheat the oven to 325 degrees.

2. While the oven is heating up use a medium bowl and add in the all-purpose flour, unsweetened cocoa, baking powder and dash of salt. Stir well to mix.

3. Add the butter into a separate medium bowl. Beat with an electric mixer on the highest setting until smooth in consistency. Add in the granulated sugar and continue to beat until fluffy in consistency. Add in the eggs and continue to beat until mixed.

4. Add in the buttermilk, instant espresso and pure vanilla. Stir well to mix.

5. Add in the flour mixture and continue to beat until evenly mixed.

6. Add in the bittersweet cacao. Fold gently to incorporate.

7. Pour the cake batter into a greased and floured Bundt pan. Place into the oven to bake for 1 hour and 25 minutes or until the cake is completely baked through. Remove and allow the cake to cool before transferring to a wire rack to cool completely.

8. Then make the chocolate glaze. To do this add in all of the ingredients for the glaze except for the vanilla into a microwave safe bowl. Microwave for 1 to 2 minutes or until the chocolate is melted. Add in the vanilla and stir well until smooth.

9. Then make the buttermilk glaze. To do this use a small bowl and add in the powdered sugar, buttermilk and pure vanilla. Whisk until smooth.

10. Pour the chocolate glaze and buttermilk glaze over the cooled cake. Allow to set for 10 minutes before serving.

Recipe 8: Chocolate Oreo Bundt Cake

This soft and moist chocolate Bundt cake is perfect to serve when you are having a sudden craving for chocolate. Stuffed with Oreo Cookies and topped off with Oreo icing, this is a dish even the pickiest of children will love.

Yield: 10 to 12 Servings

Cooking Time: 1 Hour and 10 Minutes

Ingredients for the cake:

- 12 Oreos, crushed
- 2 ¾ cups of self-rising flour
- 1 teaspoon of baking soda
- ½ cup of cocoa, powdered
- ½ teaspoons of salt
- ½ cup of butter, unsalted
- 2 ¼ cups of sugar, granulated
- 1 cup of vegetable oil
- 2 eggs, large
- 2 teaspoons of pure vanilla
- 1 cup of buttermilk

Ingredients for the glaze:

- 2 ½ cups of sugar, powdered
- 3 tablespoons of milk, whole
- ½ teaspoons of pure vanilla
- 4 to 5 Oreo Cookies, crushed and for topping

AAAAAAAAAAAAAAAAAAAAAAAAAAAAAAAAAAAAAAAAAAAAAAAAAAA

Instructions:

1. First heat up the oven to 350 degrees. While the oven is heating up grease a large Bundt pan with cooking spray. Dust the Bundt pan with the powdered cocoa and set aside.

2. Using a large bowl, add in the self-rising flour, baking soda, powdered cocoa and dash of salt. Stir well to mix and set aside.

3. Add the butter to a large bowl. Beat with an electric mixer until creamy in consistency. Add in the granulated sugar, vegetable oil, large eggs and pure vanilla. Beat again until fluffy in consistency.

4. Add the flour mixture to this mixture. Add in the buttermilk and beat on the lowest setting with the electric mixer until mixed. Add in the Oreo's and fold to incorporate.

5. Pour the batter into the prepared Bundt pan. Place into the oven to bake for 1 hour or until completely baked through. Remove and allow to cool in the pan for 20 minutes before inverting and set aside to cool completely.

6. While the cake is cooling prepare the glaze. To do this add the powdered sugar, whole milk and pure vanilla into a small bowl. Beat with a whisk until smooth in consistency.

7. Pour the glaze over the Bundt cake and garnish with the crushed Oreo cookies. Serve immediately.

Recipe 9: Apple and Cream Cheese Bundt Cake

This is a great tasting Bundt cake that you can make for the Thanksgiving holiday. Featuring a cream cheese filling and a praline frosting, this is a dish you won't be able to get enough of.

Yield: 12 Servings

Cooking Time: 4 Hours and 10 Minutes

Ingredients for the cream cheese filling:

- 1, 8 -ounce pack of cream cheese, soft
- ¼ cup of butter, soft
- ½ cup of sugar, granulated
- 1 egg, large
- 2 tablespoons of flour, all-purpose
- 1 teaspoon of pure vanilla

Ingredients for the apple cake batter:

- 1 cup of pecans, chopped
- 3 cups of all-purpose flour
- 1 cup of sugar, granulated
- 1 cup of brown sugar, light and packed
- 2 teaspoons of cinnamon
- 1 teaspoon of salt
- 1 teaspoon of baker's style baking soda
- 1 teaspoon of nutmeg
- ½ teaspoons of allspice
- 3 eggs, beaten lightly
- ¾ cup of canola oil
- ¾ cup of applesauce
- 1 teaspoon of pure vanilla
- 3 cups of gala apples, peeled and chopped

Ingredients for the praline frosting:

- ½ cup of brown sugar, light and packed
- ¼ cup of butter
- 3 tablespoons of milk, whole
- 1 teaspoon of pure vanilla
- 1 cup of sugar, powdered

AA

Instructions:

1. First make the filling. To do this add the soft cream cheese, soft butter and granulated sugar into a medium bowl. Beat with an electric mixer until evenly mixed. Add in the large egg, all-purpose flour and pure vanilla. Beat until smooth in consistency.

2. Then preheat the oven to 350 degrees. While the oven is heating up place the chopped pecans onto a large baking pan and place into the oven to bake for 8 to 10 minutes or until toasted. Remove and set aside.

3. In a large bowl add in the all-purpose flour and the remaining ingredients for the batter except for the gala apples. Stir well until smooth and just moist. Add in the toasted pecans and chopped apples. Fold to incorporate.

4. Pour 2/3 of the apple mixture into a large greased and floured Bundt pan. Pour the cream cheese filling over the apple mixture. Swirl the filling around and pour the remaining apple mixture over the filling.

5. Place into the oven to bake for 1 hour and 15 minutes or until the cake is fully baked through. Remove and allow the cake to cool for 10 minutes before transferring to a wire rack to cool completely.

6. While the cake is cooling prepare the frosting. To do this use a medium saucepan and set over medium heat. Add in the light brown sugar, butter and whole milk. Whisk to mix and bring to a boil. Allow to boil for 1 minute.

7. Remove from heat and add in the pure vanilla. Stir well to mix.

8. Add in the powdered sugar. Whisk until smooth in consistency. Allow to sit for 5 minutes or until thick in consistency.

9. Pour the glaze over the cooled cake. Allow to set for 5 minutes before serving.

Recipe 10: Coconut Bundt Cake

This is a delicious Bundt cake that is simply out of this world. Moist with every bite and packed full of a delicious coconut flavor, this is one dish I know you will want to make during the holiday season or for Mother's Day.

Yield: 12 Servings

Cooking Time: 1 Hour and 20 Minutes

Ingredients for the cake:

- 1 ½ cups of butter, soft
- 2 cups of sugar, granulated
- 4 eggs, large
- 1 cup of sour cream
- ½ teaspoons of baking powder
- 1 teaspoon of coconut extract
- 1 ¾ cups of all-purpose flour
- 2 cups of coconut, flaked

Ingredients for the coconut glaze:

- 1 cup of sugar, powdered
- ¼ cup of heavy cream
- 1 teaspoon of coconut extract
- ½ cup of coconut, flaked and optional

Instructions:

1. First heat up the oven to 325 degrees. While the oven is heating up grease and flour a large Bundt pan.

2. Then use a medium bowl and add in the all-purpose flour and flaked coconut. Stir well to mix and set aside.

3. Use a separate large bowl and add in the butter and granulated sugar. Beat with an electric mixer on the highest setting until creamy in consistency. Add in the large eggs, sour cream, baking powder and coconut extract. Continue to beat until fluffy in consistency.

4. Add the flour mixture to this mixture. Stir well until evenly combined. Allow the batter to rest for 5 minutes.

5. Pour the batter into the prepared Bundt cake pan. Place into the oven to bake for 1 hour and 10 minutes or until the Bundt cake is fully baked through. Remove and allow to cool in the pan for 25 minutes. After this time invert the cake and set aside to cool completely.

6. While the cake is cooling, make the glaze. To do this add all the ingredients for the glaze to a medium bowl. Whisk until smooth in consistency. Pour the glaze over the top and allow to drizzle down the sides.

7. Top off with the flaked coconut and serve.

Recipe 11: Brown Sugar and Bourbon Bundt Cake

There is no other sweet tasting Bundt cake quite like this one. Packed full with plenty of brown sugar and bourbon, this recipe is sweet but has a bit of a kick.

Yield: 12 Servings

Cooking Time: 2 Hours and 35 Minutes

List of Ingredients:

- 1 cup of butter, soft
- ½ cup of shortening
- 1, 16 -ounce pack of brown sugar, light and packed
- 5 eggs, large
- 1, 5 -ounce can of milk, evaporated
- ½ cup of bourbon
- 3 cups of all-purpose flour
- ½ teaspoons of baking powder
- ½ teaspoons of salt
- 1 tablespoon of vanilla bean paste
- 2 tablespoons of sugar, powdered
- Candied oranges, for garnish
- Magnolia leaves, for garnish

AAAAAAAAAAAAAAAAAAAAAAAAAAAAAAAAAAAAAAAAAAAAAAAAAAAA

Instructions:

1. First heat up the oven to 325 degrees.

2. While the oven is heating up, place the butter and shortening in a large bowl and then beat with an electric mixer until creamy in consistency.

3. Add in the light brown sugar and continue to beat until creamy in consistency. Add in the eggs and beat until incorporate.

4. In a separate medium bowl add in the evaporated milk and bourbon. Stir thoroughly to combine.

5. Using a separate large bowl add in the all-purpose flour, baking powder and dash of salt. Stir well to mix. Add this mixture to the butter mixture. Add the evaporated milk mixture into the butter mixture as well. Beat on the lowest setting with an electric mixer until well blended.

6. Add in the vanilla bean paste and stir well until incorporated.

7. Pour the batter into a large greased and floured Bundt pan.

8. Place into the oven to bake for 1 hour and 10 minutes or until the cake is completely baked through. Then move it to a wire rack to completely cool.

9. Sprinkle powdered sugar over the top and garnish with the candied oranges and magnolia leaves.

Recipe 12: Cinnamon Roll Bundt Cake

If you are a huge fan of cinnamon rolls, then this is the perfect Bundt cake for you to make. Serve this in the morning for a tasty treat to help you kickstart your day.

Yield: 8 to 10 Servings

Cooking Time: 1 Hour and 10 Minutes

Ingredients for the cake:

- 1 pack of yellow cake mix
- 2 tablespoons of brown sugar, light and packed
- 2 teaspoons of cinnamon
- ¼ teaspoons of nutmeg
- 1 ¼ cups of pecans, chopped and divided
- 1 cup of sour cream
- 1/3 cup of vegetable oil
- ¼ cup of water
- 3 tablespoons of honey
- 4 eggs, large
- 1 teaspoon of pure vanilla

Ingredients for the glaze:

- 4 -ounces of cream cheese, soft
- 2 cups of sugar, powdered
- 1 teaspoon of pure vanilla
- 1 to 2 tablespoons of milk, whole

AAAAAAAAAAAAAAAAAAAAAAAAAAAAAAAAAAAAAAAAAAAAAAAAAAAA

Instructions:

1. Heat up the oven to 350 degrees. While the oven is heating up grease and flour a large Bundt cake pan. Set aside.

2. Next, make the streusel filling. To do this add two tablespoons of the cake mix, light brown sugar, ground cinnamon, nutmeg and one cup of the pecans to a small bowl. Stir well until evenly mixed. Set aside.

3. Then make the batter. To do this add the remaining cake mix, vegetable oil, sour cream, honey, large eggs and pure vanilla to a large bowl. Beat with an electric mixer on the lowest setting for 2 minutes or until the batter is smooth in consistency.

4. Pour half of the batter into the bottom of the prepared pan. Sprinkle the streusel filling over the top and top off with the remaining batter.

5. Place into the oven to bake for 50 minutes or until completely baked through. After this time remove the cake from the oven and allow it to cool for about 10 minutes in the pan before removing from the pan and allowing the cake to cool completely.

6. While the cake is cooling make the glaze. To do this use a large bowl and add in the cream cheese, powdered sugar, pure vanilla and milk. Whisk until smooth in consistency.

7. Drizzle the glaze over the cake.

8. Sprinkle the reserved pecans over the cake and serve.

Recipe 13: Apple Spice Bundt Cake with Caramel Frosting

This is an old fashioned Southern cake that you can make during the autumn season. Serve a slice of this delicious cake with a cup of freshly brewed tea or coffee for the tastiest results.

Yield: 12 Servings

Cooking Time: 3 Hours and 45 Minutes

Ingredients for the cream cheese filling:

- 1, 8 -ounce pack of cream cheese, soft
- ¼ cup of sugar, granulated
- 1 egg, large
- 2 tablespoons of flour, all-purpose
- 1 teaspoon of pure vanilla

Ingredients for the batter:

- 1 cup of brown sugar, light and packed
- 1 cup of vegetable oil
- ½ cup of sugar, granulated
- 3 eggs, large
- 2 teaspoons of pure vanilla
- 2 teaspoons of baker's style baking powder
- 2 teaspoons of pumpkin pie spice, powdered
- 1 ½ teaspoons of cardamom
- 1 teaspoon of salt
- ½ teaspoons of baker's style baking soda
- ½ teaspoons of coriander
- 3 cups of flour, all-purpose
- 3 granny smith apples, peeled and finely grated
- 2/3 cup of pecans, lightly toasted and chopped

Ingredients for the caramel frosting:

- ½ cup of brown sugar, light and packed
- ¼ cup of heavy cream
- ¼ cup of butter, salted
- 1 teaspoon of pure vanilla
- 1 ¼ cups of sugar, powdered

Instructions:

1. First heat up the oven to 350 degrees.

2. While the oven is heating up add the cream cheese, sugar, large egg, all-purpose flour and pure vanilla to a medium bowl. Beat until smooth in consistency.

3. Then prepare the batter. To do this use a large bowl and add in the light brown sugar, vegetable oil and sugar. Beat until evenly mixed. Then add in the eggs and pure vanilla. Beat again.

4. In a separate bowl add in the baker's style baking powder, pumpkin pie spice, ground cardamom, dash of salt, baker's style baking soda, ground coriander and three cups of flour. Stir well to mix and add into the brown sugar mixture. Beat with an electric mixer on the lowest setting.

5. Add in the apples and fold gently until incorporated.

6. Spoon half of the batter into a large greased Bundt pan. Drop a dollop of the cream cheese filling over the batter. Swirl the filling around using a butter knife. Pour the remaining batter over the filling.

7. Place into the oven to bake for 1 hour or until completely baked through. Remove and transfer the cake to a wire rack to cool completely.

8. While the cake is cooling make the frosting. To do this place a medium saucepan over medium heat. Add in the light brown sugar, heavy cream and butter. Bring this mixture to a boil and allow to boil for one minute.

9. Remove the pan from heat and add in the pure vanilla. Stir well to mix. Add in the powdered sugar and whisk until smooth in consistency. Set aside for 5 minutes, until thick in consistency.

10. Drizzle the frosting over the top of the cake and garnish with the chopped pecans. Serve immediately.

Recipe 14: Orange Creamsicle Bundt Cake

This is one Bundt cake recipe that you can make to reminisce about your childhood. Made with creamy vanilla icing and zesty orange flavor, this will soon become one of your favorite treats.

Yield: 16 Servings

Cooking Time: 1 Hour and 20 Minutes

Ingredients for the cake:

- 1 cup of unsalted butter, soft
- 1 ½ cups of sugar, granulated
- 3 eggs, large
- 2 teaspoons of pure vanilla
- 1/3 cup of orange juice, fresh and squeezed
- 2 tablespoons of orange zest, grated
- 2 ½ cups of all-purpose flour
- 1 teaspoon of baking powder
- ½ teaspoons of salt
- 1 1/3 cup of milk, 2%
- 4 -ounces of white chocolate, melted

Ingredients for the icing:

- 1 cup of sugar, powdered
- 2 teaspoons of pure vanilla
- 1 to 1 ½ tablespoons of milk, whole
- Orange zest, fresh and for garnish

AAAAAAAAAAAAAAAAAAAAAAAAAAAAAAAAAAAAAAAAAAAAAAAAAAAA

Instructions:

1. First heat up the oven to 350 degrees. While the oven is heating up grease and flour a large Bundt pan.

2. Then use a small bowl and add in the white chocolate. Microwave from 30 seconds to 1 minute or until fully melted and smooth in consistency. Remove and set aside to cool.

3. Use a medium bowl and add in the all-purpose flour, baking powder and a dash of salt. Stir well to mix and set aside.

4. Add the butter and sugar to a large bowl. Use an electric mixer and beat until creamy in consistency. Add in the eggs, pure vanilla, fresh orange juice and orange zest. Beat again to mix.

5. Add the flour mixture into this creamy mixture as well as the milk. Add in the melted chocolate and beat until evenly mixed.

6. Pour the batter into the Bundt pan.

7. Place into the oven to bake for 1 hour or until completely baked through. Remove and transfer to a wire rack to cool completely.

8. While the cake is cooling, prepare the icing. To do this use a medium bowl and add in the pure vanilla and powdered sugar. Whisk until smooth in consistency.

9. Pour the icing over the Bundt pan, allowing it to drizzle over the side. Serve with a garnish of fresh orange zest.

Recipe 15: Red Velvet Marble Bundt Cake

If you love the taste of red velvet cake, then this is the perfect Bundt cake for you. Make this for the holiday season to make a treat nobody will be able to resist.

Yield: 10 to 12 Servings

Cooking Time: 2 Hours and 45 Minutes

List of Ingredients:

- 1 cup of butter, soft
- ½ cup of shortening
- 2 ½ cups of sugar
- 6 eggs, large
- 3 cups of all-purpose flour
- 1 teaspoon of baker's style baking powder
- ½ teaspoons of salt
- ¾ cup of whole milk
- 1 teaspoon of pure vanilla
- 1 tablespoon of cocoa, unsweetened
- 1 tablespoon of red food coloring
- Mint sprigs, for garnish

Ingredients for the vanilla glaze:

- 2 ½ cups of sugar, powdered
- 3 tablespoons + 1 teaspoon of milk, whole
- 1 teaspoon of pure vanilla

AAAAAAAAAAAAAAAAAAAAAAAAAAAAAAAAAAAAAAAAAAAAAAAAAAAAAA

Instructions:

1. First heat up the oven to 325 degrees.

2. While the oven is heating up place the butter and shortening in a large bowl. Beat with an electric mixer on the highest setting until creamy in consistency. Add in the sugar and continue to beat until fluffy in consistency. Add in the eggs and continue to beat until blended.

3. In a separate large bowl add in the all-purpose flour, baking powder and dash of salt. Stir well to mix and add into the butter mixture. Beat on the lowest setting until blended. Add in the vanilla and beat to incorporate.

4. Pour 2 ½ cups of the batter into a medium bowl. Add in the unsweetened cocoa and red food coloring. Stir well until blended.

5. Add two scoops of the plain batter into a large greased and floured Bundt pan. Add a scoop of the red velvet batter. Repeat these layers until both batters have been used.

6. Place into the oven to bake for 1 hour and 5 minutes or until the cake is completely baked through. Remove and transfer to a wire rack to cool completely.

7. While the cake is cooling make the vanilla glaze. To do this add the powdered sugar, whole milk and pure vanilla to a small bowl. Whisk until smooth in consistency. Pour the glaze over the cake and serve immediately.

Recipe 16: Dark Chocolate Peanut Butter Bundt Cake

This is a cake that you can make whenever you have the need to spoil yourself. Smothered in peanut butter and chocolate, this is a great dish to make whenever you have a cheat day.

Yield: 8 Servings

Cooking Time: 1 Hour

Ingredients for the cake:

- 1 box of dark chocolate fudge cake mix
- One 3 1/2 -ounce box of instant pudding mix
- 4 eggs, large
- 1 cup of sour cream, low in fat
- ¼ cup of vegetable oil
- ½ cup of miniature chocolate chips, semisweet
- 1 cup of peanut butter chips

Ingredients for the topping:

- 4 -ounces of baking chocolate, semisweet and broken into small pieces
- ¼ cup of heavy cream
- 2 tablespoons of butter
- 1/3 cup of peanut butter, creamy

Instructions:

1. First prepare the cake. To do this heat up the oven to 350 degrees.

2. While the oven is heating up use a large bowl and add in the chocolate fudge cake mix, pudding mix, large eggs, sour cream, vegetable oil, semisweet chocolate chips and peanut butter chips. Stir well to mix.

3. Grease a large Bundt cake pan with cooking spray and then pour the batter in.

4. Place into the oven to bake for 45 to 50 minutes or until completely baked through. Remove and transfer to a wire rack to cool for 10 minutes. Invert the cake onto the rack to cool completely.

5. While the cake is cooling, make the topping. To do this use a small bowl and add in the baking chocolate pieces, heavy cream and butter. Melt in the microwave for 30 seconds to 1 minute or until fully melted. Stir until smooth.

6. Pour the topping over the cooled Bundt cake.

7. Then use another small bowl and add in the peanut butter. Microwave for 30 seconds or until melted. Drizzle over the cake.

8. Allow the cake to set for 15 minutes or until the topping is set. Serve.

Recipe 17: Vanilla Butter Bundt Cake

This is a great tasting Bundt cake that you can make if you want a simple cake to enjoy. Packed with plenty of vanilla flavor, I know this is one cake you will want to make as often as possible.

Yield: 12 Servings

Cooking Time: 2 Hours and 15 Minutes

Ingredients for the cake:

- 1 cup of butter, soft
- 2 ½ cups of sugar
- 5 eggs, large
- 3 cups of all-purpose flour
- 1 teaspoon of baking powder
- ¼ teaspoons of salt
- ¾ cup of half and half
- 1 tablespoon of pure vanilla

Ingredients for the white icing:

- 2 cups of sugar, powdered
- 3 to 4 tablespoons of milk, whole
- 1 teaspoon of pure vanilla
- 1 teaspoon of meringue, powdered

Instructions:

1. Add the butter to a large bowl and beat with an electric mixer on the highest setting until creamy in consistency. Add in the sugar and eggs. Continue to beat until fluffy in consistency.

2. In a separate large bowl add in the all-purpose flour, baking powder and dash of salt. Stir to mix and add this mixture to the butter mixture. Beat on the lowest setting until evenly blended.

3. Add in the pure vanilla and stir to incorporate.

4. Pour the batter into a large greased and floured Bundt pan.

5. Place into the oven to bake for 1 hour and 10 minutes or until completely baked through. Remove and transfer to a wire rack to cool completely.

6. While the cake is cooling make the frosting. To do this add all the ingredients for the frosting to a small bowl. Beat with an electric mixer on the highest setting until fluffy in consistency. Pour over the cooled cake and serve.

Recipe 18: Dr. Pepper Bundt Cake

This Dr. Pepper Bundt cake is made using Cherry Dr. Pepper, giving it a tasty cherry flavor that I know you will love. Make this dish whenever you are craving something sweet to enjoy.

Yield: 16 Servings

Cooking Time: 1 Hour

List of Ingredients:

- 2 sticks of unsalted butter, melted
- 2 ¾ cups of all-purpose flour
- 1 teaspoon of baking soda
- ½ teaspoons of salt
- 2 cups of sugar, granulated
- 2 eggs, large
- 1 teaspoon of vanilla, pure
- 1 cup of Cherry Dr. Pepper
- 2 tablespoons of cherry juice
- 1 cup of sour cream
- ½ cup of Maraschino cherries, optional
- Sugar, powdered and for dusting

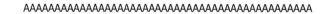

Instructions:

1. First heat up the oven to 325 degrees. While the oven is heating up grease and flour a large Bundt pan.

2. Place the all-purpose flour, baking soda and salt in a small bowl. Stir to mix and set aside.

3. Add the sugar and melted butter to a medium bowl. Beat with an electric mixer until smooth in consistency. Add in the large eggs and pure vanilla. Continue to beat until mixed. This should take one minute.

4. Add in the Cherry Dr. Pepper and maraschino cherry juice. Continue to mix until incorporated.

5. Add in the flour mixture and beat on the lowest setting until evenly mixed.

6. Add in the sour cream and Maraschino cherries. Fold to incorporate.

7. Pour the batter into the prepared Bundt pan.

8. Place into the oven to bake for 50 minutes or until completely baked through. Remove and allow to cool completely.

9. Dust with the powdered sugar and serve.

Recipe 19: Chocolate Chip Bundt Cake

If you love the taste of chocolate chip cookies, then this is one homemade Bundt cake I know you are going to fall in love with. It is perfect to make for a person's birthday party, or even serve as a holiday treat.

Yield: 12 Servings

Cooking Time: 2 Hours

List of Ingredients:

- 2/3 cup of pecans, chopped
- ¼ cup of butter, soft
- 2 tablespoons of sugar, granulated
- 2 ¾ cups of all-purpose flour
- 1 teaspoon of baking soda
- 1 teaspoon of salt
- 1 cup of butter, soft
- 1 cup of brown sugar, light and packed
- ½ cup of sugar, granulated
- 1 tablespoon of pure vanilla
- 4 eggs, large
- 1 cup of buttermilk
- 1, 12 -ounce pack of semi-sweet chocolate
- Whipped cream, for garnish
- Cherries, fresh and for garnish

Instructions:

1. First heat up the oven to 350 degrees.

2. While the oven is heating up add the chopped pecans, soft butter and granulated sugar to a small bowl. Stir well with a fork and sprinkle into a large floured and greased Bundt pan.

3. Use a separate large bowl and add in the all-purpose flour, baking soda and dash of salt.

4. Add the soft butter, light brown sugar, white sugar and pure vanilla to a medium bowl. Beat with an electric mixer for 5 minutes or until fluffy in consistency. Add in the eggs and continue to beat until blended.

5. Add in the all-purpose flour mixture and continue to beat until incorporate.

6. Add in the chocolate and fold to incorporate.

7. Pour the batter into the prepared Bundt pan.

8. Place into the oven to bake for 1 hour or until the cake is completely baked through. Remove and transfer to a wire rack to cool. Garnish with the whipped cream and cherries before serving.

Recipe 20: Rum Glazed Sweet Potato Bundt Cakes

These miniature Bundt cakes are perfect to serve during the Thanksgiving season. Made with pureed sweet potatoes, raisins and plenty of rum, this is a tasty treat for any holiday party you may attend.

Yield: 36 Servings

Cooking Time: 1 Hour and 15 Minutes

List of Ingredients:

- ¾ cup of raisins, golden
- 1/3 cup of rum, dark
- 4 eggs, large
- 2 cups of sugar, granulated
- 1 cup of vegetable oil
- 2 teaspoons of pure vanilla
- 2 cups of sweet potatoes, roasted and pureed
- 3 cups of all-purpose flour
- 1 ½ teaspoons of cinnamon
- 1 teaspoon of baking powder
- 1 teaspoon of baking soda
- ½ teaspoons of sea salt
- ½ teaspoons of nutmeg
- ¾ cup of buttermilk
- ½ cup of brown sugar, light and packed
- ¼ cup of butter
- 3 tablespoons of whipping cream
- ½ cup of pecans, lightly toasted and chopped

AAAAAAAAAAAAAAAAAAAAAAAAAAAAAAAAAAAAAAAAAAAAAAAAAAAA

Instructions:

1. In a medium bowl add in the golden raisins and dark rum. Stir to mix and allow to stand for 30 minutes.

2. During this time use a large bowl and add in the large eggs and granulated sugar. Beat with an electric mixer until thick in consistency. Add in the vegetable oil, pure vanilla and sweet potato puree. Continue to beat until evenly mixed.

3. Preheat the oven to 350 degrees.

4. While the oven is heating up use a separate large bowl and add in the all-purpose flour, nutmeg, the dash of sea salt and baking powder and soda. Stir well to mix. Pour this mixture into the egg mixture along with the buttermilk. Beat with an electric mixer on the lowest setting until mixed.

5. Drain the raisins from the rum, making sure to set the rum aside to reserve. Add the raisins to the batter and fold to incorporate.

6. Pour the cake batter into three large Bundt brownie pans that have been greased and floured, making sure to fill it ¾ of the way.

7. Place into the oven to bake for 15 minutes or until completely baked through. Remove and set onto a wire rack to cool completely.

8. While the cakes are in the oven, place a large saucepan over medium to high heat. Add in the light brown sugar, butter and heavy whipping cream. Stir to mix and bring this mixture to a boil. Allow to boil for 3 minutes or until the mixture is thick in consistency. Remove from heat and add in the reserved rum. Stir to incorporate.

9. Pierce the top of the cakes with a wooden toothpick. Dip the top portions of the cakes into the glaze. Place onto a wire rack with the glaze side facing up.

10. Sprinkle the pecans over the top and serve.

Recipe 21: Tennessee Jam Bundt Cake

This is the perfect Bundt recipe to make during the summer season. Packed full of delicious berry jam taste, this is one dish you can bring on your next family picnic to help satisfy everyone's sweet tooth.

Yield: 12 Servings

Cooking Time: 4 Hours and 30 Minutes

Ingredients for the cake:

- 1 ½ cups of pecans, chopped
- 1 ½ cups of sugar, granulated
- 1 cup of butter, soft
- 4 eggs, large
- 3 cups of all-purpose flour
- 2 tablespoons of cocoa, unsweetened
- 1 teaspoon of cinnamon
- ½ teaspoons of salt
- ½ teaspoons of allspice
- ¼ teaspoons of nutmeg
- 1 cup of buttermilk
- 1 teaspoon of baking soda
- 1 ½ cups of blackberry jam, seedless
- 2 teaspoons of pure vanilla
- Shortening

Ingredients for the caramel frosting:

- ½ cup of brown sugar, light and packed
- ¼ cup of whipping cream
- ¼ cup of butter
- 1 teaspoon of pure vanilla
- 1 ¼ cups of sugar, powdered
- Blackberries, fresh and for garnish
- Mint leaves, fresh and for garnish

Instructions:

1. First heat up the oven to 350 degrees. While the oven is heating up place the pecans in a single layer into a large pan. Place into the oven to bake for 10 minutes or until lightly toasted. Remove and set on a wire rack to cool.

2. Reduce the temperature in the oven to 325 degrees.

3. Using a large bowl, add in the eggs, granulated sugar and butter. Beat with an electric mixer until fluffy in consistency.

4. Use a separate large bowl and add in the all-purpose flour, unsweetened cocoa, ground cinnamon, dash of salt, ground allspice and ground nutmeg. Stir well to mix.

5. In a separate medium bowl add in the buttermilk and baking soda. Stir to mix. Add in the flour mixture and stir well until just mixed.

6. Add in the butter mixture and beat with an electric mixer until blended. Add in the jam, pure vanilla and lightly toasted pecans. Beat until incorporated.

7. Pour the batter into a large greased and floured Bundt pan.

8. Place into the oven to bake for 1 hour and 15 minutes or until completely baked through. Remove and set aside on a wire rack to cool completely.

9. While the cake is cooling make the frosting. To do this add the light and packed brown sugar, heavy whipping cream and soft butter to a medium saucepan set over medium heat. Bring this mixture to a boil and whisk while boiling for 1 minutes.

10. Remove the mixture from heat and add in the pure vanilla and powdered sugar. Whisk to mix until smooth in consistency.

11. Allow to cool for 5 minutes or until thick in consistency. Pour over the cooled cake and serve.

Recipe 22: Miniature Bourbon and Cola Bundt Cakes

These are the perfect cakes to make and serve at your next cocktail party. Made with a sweet bourbon and cola glaze, these miniature cakes will be gone in just a matter of minutes.

Yield: 36 Servings

Cooking Time: 1 Hour and 40 Minutes

Ingredients for the cake:

- 1 ½ cups of butter, soft
- 2 ½ cups of sugar
- 3 eggs, large
- 1 ½ teaspoons of pure vanilla
- 1 cup of cola
- ¾ cup of buttermilk
- ½ cup of bourbon
- 3 cups of all-purpose flour
- ½ cup of cocoa, unsweetened
- 1 ½ teaspoons of baking soda
- ½ teaspoons of salt

Ingredients for the bourbon and cola glaze:

- ¼ cup of butter
- 3 tablespoons of cola
- 2 ½ tablespoons of cocoa, unsweetened
- 1 tablespoon of bourbon
- 2 cups + 2 tablespoons of sugar, powdered

Instructions:

1. First heat up the oven to 350 degrees.

2. While the oven is heating up add the butter to a large bowl. Beat with an electric mixer on the highest setting until creamy in consistency. Add in the sugar, large eggs and pure vanilla. Continue to beat until evenly blended.

3. In a small bowl add in the cola, buttermilk and bourbon. Stir well to mix.

4. In a separate large bowl add in the all-purpose flour, unsweetened cocoa, baking soda and dash of salt. Stir well to mix.

5. Pour in the cola mixture and beat on the lowest setting until evenly blended.

6. Pour the batter into 12 cup Bundt brownie pans, making sure to only fill ¾ of the way with the batter.

7. Place into the oven to bake for 15 minutes or until completely baked through. Remove and set onto a wire rack to cool completely.

8. While the cakes are cooling prepare the bourbon and cola glaze. To do this place a medium saucepan over low to medium heat. Add in the butter, cola and unsweetened cocoa. Stir well to mix and cook for 1 minute or until the butter melts.

9. Remove from heat and add in the bourbon and powdered sugar. Beat with an electric mixer on the highest setting until smooth in consistency.

10. Pour the glaze over the cooled cake. Serve.

Recipe 23: Dark Chocolate Bundt Cake

This is a delicious Bundt cake that every chocoholic is going to love. It is not only beautiful to look at, but it is also beautiful to eat.

Yield: 12 Servings

Cooking Time: 2 Hours and 25 Minutes

Ingredients for the cake:

- 8 -ounces of chocolate, semisweet and chopped
- 1, 16 -ounce can of chocolate syrup
- 1 cup of butter, soft
- 4 eggs, large
- 2 ½ cups of all-purpose flour
- ½ teaspoons of baker's style baking soda
- ¼ teaspoons of salt
- 1 cup of buttermilk
- 1 teaspoon of pure vanilla

Ingredients for the icing:

- 2 cups of sugar, powdered
- 3 to 4 tablespoons of milk, whole
- 1 teaspoon of pure vanilla

AAAAAAAAAAAAAAAAAAAAAAAAAAAAAAAAAAAAAAAAAAAAAAAAAAA

Instructions:

1. First place the chocolate into a small microwave safe bowl. Microwave for 30 seconds to 1 minute or until fully melted. Add in the chocolate syrup and stir until smooth in consistency. Set aside.

2. Add the butter to a large bowl. Beat until creamy in consistency. Add in the sugar and the eggs. Continue to beat until fluffy in consistency.

3. In a separate large bowl add in the all-purpose flour, baking soda and dash of salt. Stir well to mix and add into the butter mixture. Pour in the buttermilk and beat until evenly mixed.

4. Add in the pure vanilla and melted chocolate. Beat well until evenly blended.

5. Pour the batter into a large greased and floured Bundt pan.

6. Place into the oven to bake for 1 hour and 20 minutes or until completely baked through. Remove and place onto a wire rack to cool completely.

7. While the cake is cooling, make the icing. To do this add all the ingredients for the icing to a medium bowl. Whisk until smooth in consistency.

8. Pour immediately over the cooled cake and allow to rest for 5 minutes before serving.

Recipe 24: Cranberry and Apple Pumpkin Bundt Cake

This is another delicious Bundt cake recipe that you can make during the fall season. Perfect for the holidays, this is a treat the entire family can enjoy.

Yield: 12 Servings

Cooking Time: 4 Hours and 30 Minutes

Ingredients for the cake:

- ¾ cup of pecans, chopped
- 1 ½ cups of granny smith apples, peeled and diced
- 2 tablespoons of butter, melted
- ½ cup of cranberries, sweetened, dried and chopped
- ½ cup of brown sugar, light and packed
- 3 tablespoons of all-purpose flour
- 2 cups of sugar, granulated
- 1 cup of butter, soft
- 4 eggs, large
- 1, 15 -ounce can of pumpkin
- 1 tablespoon of pure vanilla
- 3 cups of all-purpose flour
- 2 teaspoons of baking powder
- 2 teaspoons of pumpkin pie spice
- ½ teaspoons of baking soda

Ingredients for the maple glaze:

- ½ cup of maple syrup, pure
- 2 tablespoons of butter
- 1 tablespoon of milk, whole
- 1 teaspoon of pure vanilla
- 1 cup of sugar, powdered

AAAAAAAAAAAAAAAAAAAAAAAAAAAAAAAAAAAAAAAAAAAAAAAAAA

Instructions:

1. First heat up the oven to 350 degrees. While the oven is heating up place the pecans in a single layer onto a large baking sheet. Place into the oven to bake for 8 to 10 minutes or until lightly toasted. Remove and set aside to cool for 15 minutes.

2. Reduce the temperature of the oven to 325 degrees.

3. In a medium bowl add in the diced apples and 2 tablespoons of melted butter. Add in the cranberries, light brown sugar, all-purpose flour and lightly toasted pecans. Stir well to mix.

4. In a separate medium bowl add in the granulated sugar and one cup of butter. Beat with an electric mixer until fluffy in consistency. Add in the eggs, pumpkin and pure vanilla. Continue to beat until evenly mixed.

5. In a large bowl add in the all-purpose flour, baking powder and soda and pumpkin pie spice. Stir well to mix and add into the butter mixture. Beat with an electric mixer on the lowest setting until mixed.

6. Pour half of the batter into a large greased and floured Bundt pan. Spoon the apple mixture over the batter. Pour the remaining batter over the apple mixture.

7. Place into the oven to bake for 1 hour and 20 minutes or until completely baked through. Remove and allow to cool on a wire rack completely.

8. While the cake is cooling make the maple glaze. To do this place a small saucepan over medium to high heat. Add in the pure maple syrup, butter and whole milk. Stir well and bring this mixture to a boil. Allow to boil for 2 minutes.

9. Remove from heat and add in the pure vanilla. Add in the powdered sugar and whisk until smooth in consistency. Set aside for 5 minutes or until thick in consistency. Pour the glaze immediately over the cooled cake. Serve.

Recipe 25: Robert E. Lee Bundt Cake

Here is another Southern inspired Bundt cake that I know you won't be able to help but fall in love with. Serve this any day of the year to make a special treat for your entire family.

Yield: 12 Servings

Cooking Time: 2 Hours and 35 Minutes

List of Ingredients:

- 1 cup of butter, soft
- ½ cup of shortening
- 3 cups of sugar, granulated
- 6 eggs, large
- 3 cups of all-purpose flour
- ½ teaspoons of baking powder
- 1/8 teaspoons of salt
- 1 cup of milk, whole
- 4 teaspoons of orange zest evenly divided
- 2 teaspoons of lemon zest, fresh and evenly divided
- ¼ cup of lemon juice, fresh
- 2 cups of sugar, powdered
- 2 to 3 tablespoons of orange juice, fresh
- Raspberries, fresh and for garnish

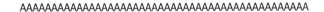

AAAAAAAAAAAAAAAAAAAAAAAAAAAAAAAAAAAAAAAAAAAAAAAAAA

Instructions:

1. First preheat an oven to 325 degrees.

2. While the oven is heating up add the butter and shortening to a large bowl. Beat with an electric mixer until creamy in consistency. Add in the sugar and eggs. Continue to beat until fluffy in consistency.

3. Use a large bowl and add in the all-purpose flour, baking powder and dash of salt. Stir well to mix and add to the butter mixture along with one teaspoon of the fresh orange zest, one teaspoon of the fresh lemon zest and ¼ cup of the fresh lemon juice. Beat with an electric mixer on the lowest setting until mixed.

4. Pour the batter into a large greased and floured Bundt pan.

5. Place into the oven to bake for 1 hour and 15 minutes or until completely baked through. Remove and transfer to a wire rack to cool completely.

6. After this time add the powdered sugar, fresh orange juice and remaining lemon and orange zest to a small bowl. Whisk until smooth in consistency.

7. Pour over the cooled cake and serve.

About the Author

Molly Mills always knew she wanted to feed people delicious food for a living. Being the oldest child with three younger brothers, Molly learned to prepare meals at an early age to help out her busy parents. She just seemed to know what spice went with which meat and how to make sauces that would dress up the blandest of pastas. Her creativity in the kitchen was a blessing to a family where money was tight and making new meals every day was a challenge.

Molly was also a gifted athlete as well as chef and secured a Lacrosse scholarship to Syracuse University. This was a blessing to her family as she was the first to go to college and at little cost to her parents. She took full advantage of her college education and earned a business degree. When she graduated, she joined her culinary skills and business acumen into a successful catering business. She wrote her first e-book after a customer asked if she could pay for several of her recipes. This sparked the entrepreneurial spirit in Mills and she thought if one person wanted them, then why not share the recipes with the world!

Molly lives near her family's home with her husband and three children and still cooks for her family every chance she gets. She plays Lacrosse with a local team made up of her old teammates from college and there are always some tasty nibbles on the ready after each game.

Don't Miss Out!

Scan the QR-Code below and you can sign up to receive emails whenever Molly Mills publishes a new book. There's no charge and no obligation.

Sign Me Up

https://molly.gr8.com

CPSIA information can be obtained
at www.ICGtesting.com
Printed in the USA
LVHW041223190420
654025LV00001B/245